Contents

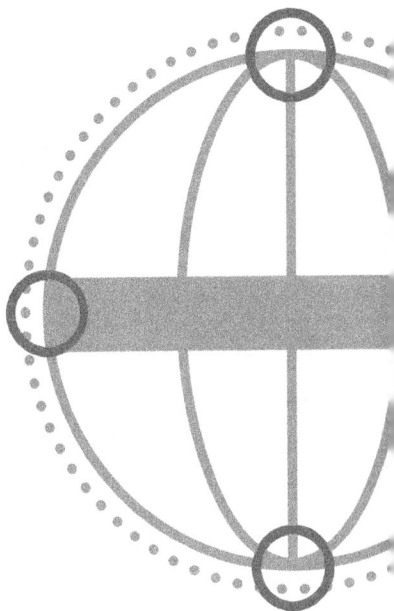

Foreword: Your Mission

So, here you are. You've arrived.

You've got the big kahuna gig that puts you exactly where you know you belong: in the driver's seat.

I won't assume the specifics of your role. You may be VP of a department, executive director of a not-for-profit, founder of a business or a C-level executive.

The million-dollar question is: how do you deliver the biggest bang possible?

At this level, the stakes are massive. Every decision you make has the potential to change people's careers and lives. Your actions can catapult the company to heights it's never known. Or depths it's feared.

But of course with big stakes come big rewards. You've got the power to chart your own course. You've got the resources and influence to pull off remarkable feats. Plus, you've got lovely perks that come with being at the top.

I want to save you the angst and agony that so many people in big jobs experience. The source of that pain is a faulty assumption that you can (and should) rely on the winning traits that brought you to glory in the first place.

Shatter that assumption. It's essential to shift your mindset and your behavior to excel at an executive level. Being top dog is not you as you were 5 years ago with a bigger title.

Some people make this shift intuitively, with no guidance at all. But most people travel a long, bumpy road before they're comfortable and successful at the top level.

My aim is to shortcut your learning with this guide to being the Ultimate Executive.

Used well, it will help you maximize your own rewards and experiences. It will maximize your impact on your organization, its employees and possibly far beyond that.

Onward, shall we?

Lisa Martin, PCC

Part One:

LEADING IS SERIOUS BUSINESS

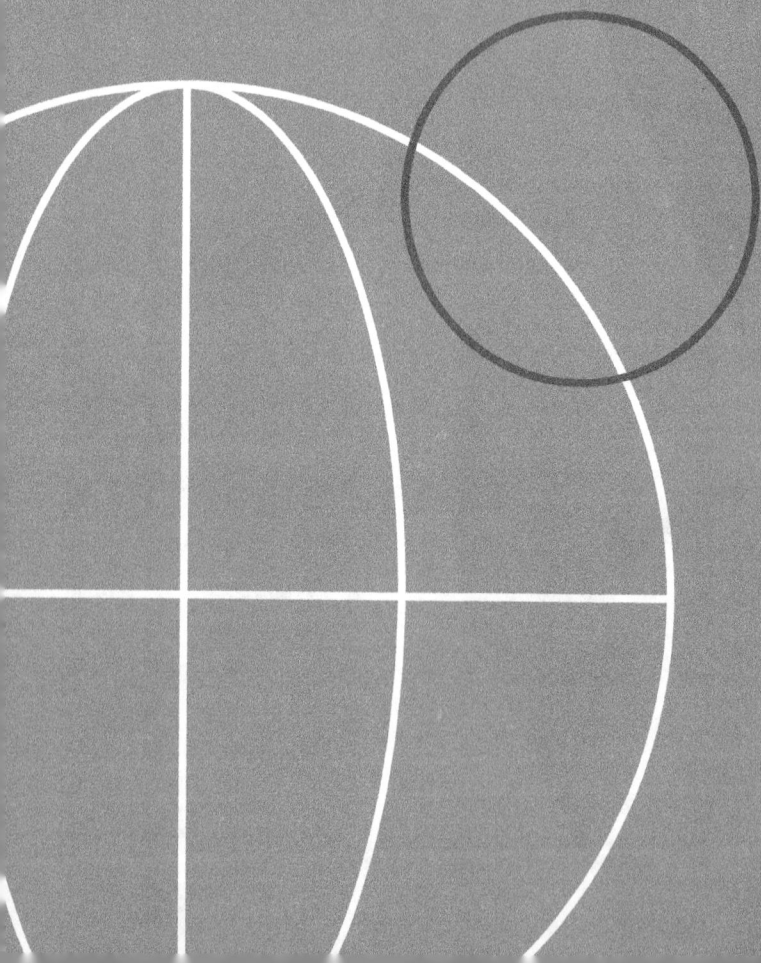

An Ultimate Executive Story

Catherine was a rock star sales manager at a mid-sized tech company. Even in a rough economy, she blew her goals out of the water every quarter. People called her 'The Closer.'

When a deal was in trouble, the higher ups called on Catherine to work her mystical powers to get the contract signed. She was a revenue-whisperer.

She loved the accolades and fully expected to be offered the top job when her boss moved on. And sure enough that's exactly what happened three years ago.

Catherine sidled into the corner office with the confidence of a star quarterback. She'd succeeded in every other job she'd ever had. It didn't occur to her there could be any other outcome.

She set to work. She spent endless days 'collaborating' with her sales managers, hounding them on the progress of every deal in the pipeline. She inserted herself into customer meetings she wasn't invited to. She 'coached' even her most senior sales reps on her personal style of pitching.

Despite all of this effort, sales were not closing. Catherine responded by frantically overseeing the creation of every proposal, often working through the night to rewrite them from scratch.

Fast-forward three months. The company suffered its worst quarter in a decade. Three stellar sales reps quit. Her department was in a shambles.

Catherine was at a loss. She'd never worked so hard in her life yet she produced a spectacular failure.

Her executive team – knowing her and believing in her – gave her one more quarter to prove her mettle. It was a gracious decision and a major gamble.

That's when I started working with Catherine, and together we realized her catastrophic quarter was the result of flying too low.

Rather than overseeing the big picture and giving her team the freedom to do their jobs, she literally tried to do their jobs for them. She relied on all of her old talents – pitching clients, writing proposals and closing deals – rather than acquiring new executive skills.

Catherine figured it out. She needed to stop pitching customers. She needed to start finding new markets for the company. And she needed to continue to use her closing skills, but now to close major partnership opportunities.

She had no choice but to quickly let go of her old ways. She shifted enough to (barely) make her numbers the following quarter. And over the next year, a full transformation occurred.

Catherine's impact on the company is now legendary. She's taken what was a regional technology company to a national stage, and she's close to signing an agreement that could open up the Asian market.

This is what happens when you're an Ultimate Executive. You have a significantly bigger impact by leaving your comfort zone and giving other people the support and freedom they need to truly shine.

Your success is now measured not just on your personal performance, but also on team and company performance.

I call this 'The Impact Effect'. It's your value proposition as a top gun.

The Evolution of an Executive

Ultimate Executives are different than RockStar Leaders.

As a RockStar Leader, individual or team performance is your primary currency. You know how to shine as a manager or an individual contributor. (See my book, *Lead: 6 Skills to Be a RockStar Leader* for more info).

Being a RockStar Leader can help you land an executive role, but it won't help you keep it.

To be an Ultimate Executive you need to deliver grand-scale, corporate-level results. This requires new skills and behaviors. It requires change. Personal change in you.

In 15 years of leadership coaching, I can tell you with certainty that people who get demoted, shunted to the bench or fired from executive jobs are those who are unwilling to embark on major personal transformation.

Don't let this be you. The hardest part is letting go of some of your most prized talents. Yes, the very skills that positioned you for executive leadership.

You need to toss some of them to the wind. Scary, yes?

Careful though. Don't chuck them all away. You'll need to examine what skills will keep you mired in detail and what skills will help you function at an executive level.

To a great extent, being an executive is about providing oversight and insight, rather than implementing the details of projects. This means you're no longer just focusing on your role and your goals.

Instead you're focusing on the bigger vision of the company, the interconnections between departments and projects, and bringing out the best in people around you.

Executive leadership is not about one department or mandate. It's about helping the company get from where it is today to where it wants to be.

Everything you do needs to be set in this broad context.

Ultimately, It's About Impact

Let's talk about The Impact Effect.

In your executive role, you can have a greater impact than ever before on your company, its employees, your community. And possibly the world. Your decisions and actions have a chain reaction, magnifying every move you make. Your status brings power and influence, if you know how to leverage it.

According to The Impact Effect, your executive role has 4 major impacts:

1 Personal Impact

2 Impact on Others

3 Impact on Your Organization

4 Possibly, Impact on the World

For you personally, your role brings the potential for serious financial reward, the power to call the shots, the freedom to do intriguing work and the possibility of reaching sizable personal and professional goals. It is the realization of a lifestyle most people only dream about.

But of course, it isn't just about you. It's also about everyone around you. Who will you hire? Promote? Fire? Whose projects will receive funding and whose budget will be cut? Who will collaborate to bring exciting new ventures to life? This is big stuff. Your choices will affect the courses of people's careers and possibly their lives.

And next, there's the effect on your organization. Your value proposition is the size and scope of your impact. Your mandate is to bring the company's most venturesome desires to reality. It's your job to discover and sponsor innovation. To plant seeds that become forests.

Being an executive means having the luxury – and responsibility – to be a long-term, visionary thinker. A strategist. You get to step beyond the everyday nuts and bolts of the business and play in the realm of ideas and possibility.

Because of this, your impact has the potential to extend beyond the reaches of your company, to your community and industry. And, if your ideas are grand enough, your impact can stretch to all corners of the globe.

Soak that in. With this level of influence, you can do great good for those around you, or you can do great harm. Weigh this with every choice you make, and be aware of the legacy you want to leave because with great influence comes great impact.

For this reason, Ultimate Executives are:

> Conscious of their impact on other people.

> Caring about their community and the world.

> Of service to the organization and its people.

> Respectful of other people's skills, talents and autonomy.

> Aware of when to lead and when to follow.

Being an Ultimate Executive is about exercising emotional intelligence, letting others shine, and making the biggest contribution you can within your company and beyond.

Part Two:

HOW TO BE THE ULTIMATE EXECUTIVE

The Method

Ultimate Executive leadership skills can be learned by anyone willing to assume the challenge of leading others to success. These skills can be learned if you're already an executive, about to be promoted or preparing for your eventual rise to the top.

The structure of this book is based on a self-coaching model that will help you develop greater self-awareness and emotional intelligence. You'll learn to apply these skills in your everyday work and life.

In this book you will find:

1 The **Ultimate Executive Model**, featuring the six skills required to be the Ultimate Executive.

2 An explanation of each **Ultimate Executive Skill** and why it matters.

3 **Four Advice Articles for each Ultimate Executive Skill** to deepen your understanding.

4 **One Leading Question for each Ultimate Executive Skill** to help you gain self-awareness.

5 **(Optional) Ultimate Executive Assessment.**

The Model

Let me introduce you to the **Ultimate Executive Model.**

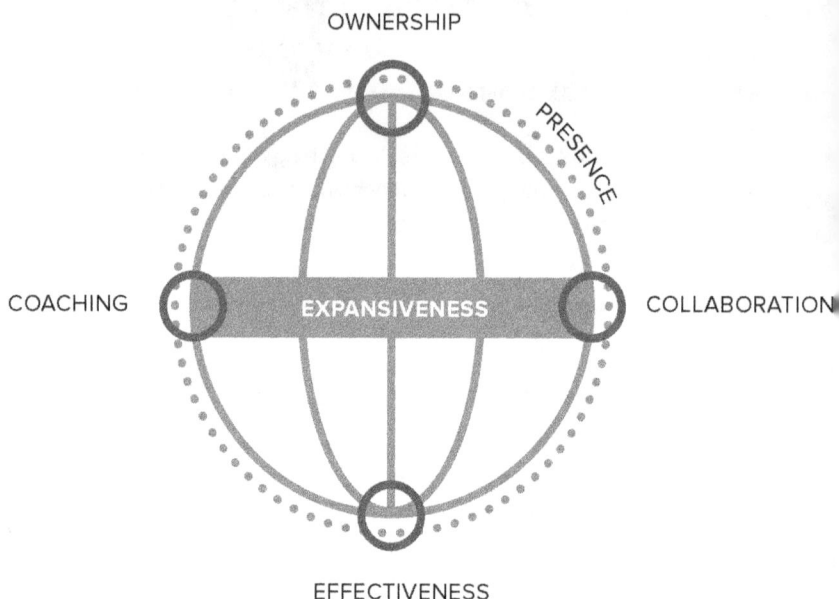

```
                    OWNERSHIP


                        ⊙
                       ╱│╲
                      ╱ │ ╲        PRESENCE
                     │  │  │
   COACHING  ⊙━━━━━━EXPANSIVENESS━━━━━⊙  COLLABORATION
                     │  │  │
                      ╲ │ ╱
                       ╲│╱
                        ⊙


                   EFFECTIVENESS
```

This model is based on 15 years of leadership coaching in a vast cross-section of industries across North America. In that time, I've delivered hundreds of workshops, coached thousands of people in senior roles and conducted in-depth interviews with countless leaders.

This model is also informed by my personal history as a corporate executive and the founder of three successful companies (see 'Acknowledgements' on page 84 for more detail).

Through all of this I've learned what distinguishes Ultimate Executives from the rest. I've seen time and time again that people who practice the following skills create major success for themselves, their organizations and beyond.

Without further ado, here are the 6 Skills to Be the Ultimate Executive:

1 **Expansiveness:** Think big and see all possibilities.

2 **Ownership:** Be ultimately accountable.

3 **Collaboration:** Possess a sharing orientation.

4 **Effectiveness:** Maximize capacity and value.

5 **Coaching:** Help others grow and succeed.

6 **Presence:** Exude the X Factor.

I encourage you to make each Ultimate Executive Skill your own, bringing it to life in a way that reflects your unique personality.

The skills require steady practice and use. They are an integrated system, so it's essential to apply them all equally. Ignoring some in favor of others will limit your ability to make a big impact.

Part Three:

THE 6 ULTIMATE EXECUTIVE SKILLS

Expansiveness

Expansiveness is thinking big. It's the ability to let your mind open up wide, seeing all possibilities and opportunities. Being an Ultimate Executive means viewing your organization from the mountain top, surveying every aspect of the landscape.

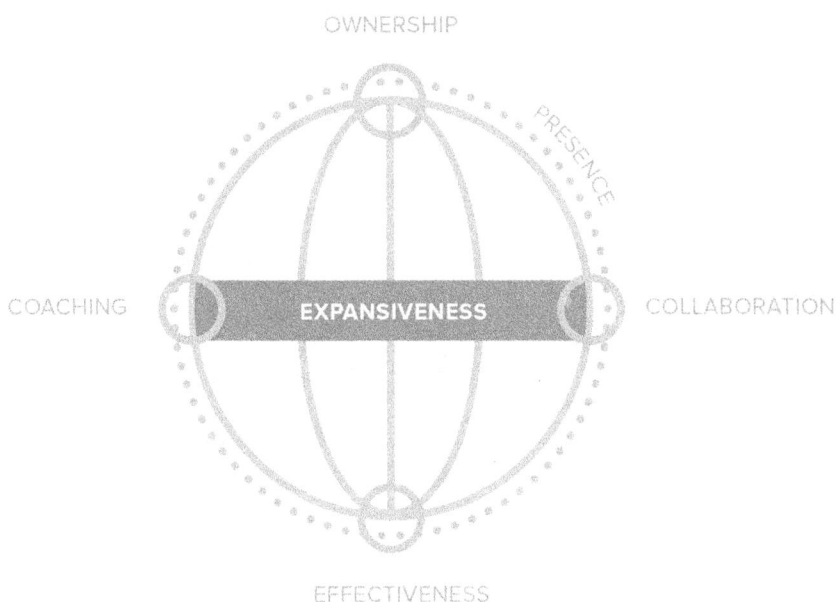

OWNERSHIP

PRESENCE

COACHING

EXPANSIVENESS

COLLABORATION

EFFECTIVENESS

Even as you manage day-to-day business, you need to ensure every initiative and task is bringing the company closer to its ultimate vision and financial goals.

If you're not constantly thinking at this level, you will find yourself bogged down. Your decisions won't factor in every vital implication. You won't have your eyes and ears tuned to changes in the market or opportunities for innovation.

The trick is – no one can give you this **expansive** view on your company. It doesn't just come with a title. This vantage point is a mental shift only you can make for yourself.

Being an Ultimate Executive is a long game. Yours is not the domain of quick wins. You need to give yourself the freedom to think far bigger, broader and more inventively than you ever have before.

To think big you need to:

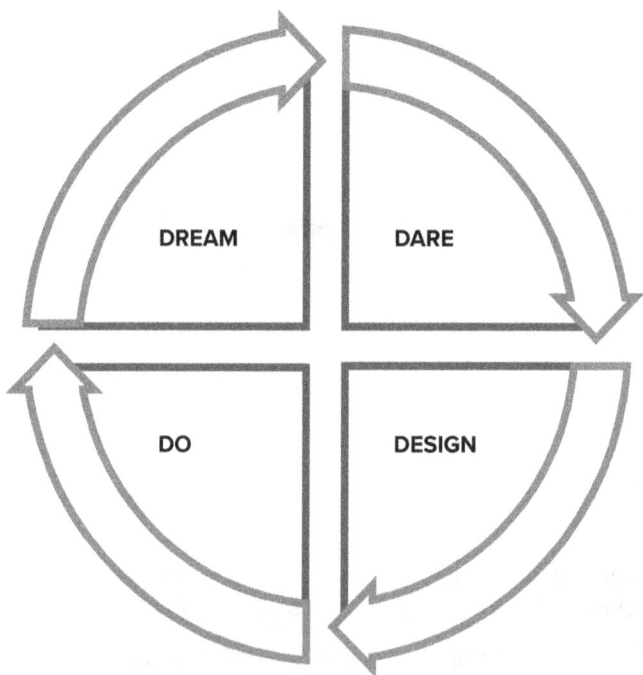

DREAM
Envision big, brassy possibilities that will improve the financial and market positions of the company. See opportunities before the rest of the market does.

DARE
Take the leap. Have the guts to take what may seem like a crazy notion to other people and make it real. Without this step, you're simply a dreamer rather than an Ultimate Executive.

DESIGN
Create a game plan for bringing your idea to life. What resources will you need? What skills will be required?

DO
Hit the road running. Share your vision, rally support, build the team, create alliances – whatever it takes to make your dream a reality. Sometimes this will be as simple as picking up the phone and scheduling a key meeting. Other times, a more complex series of steps will be needed.

One of the most exciting aspects of an executive role is having the freedom and resources to be bold. Expansiveness is about letting your adventurous, creative sides take charge. So don't hold back. You've earned the right to be audacious.

Dream Bigger

It's easy to say, 'Dream bigger,' right?

You wouldn't have gotten where you are in life if you didn't have the capacity to dream. So how do you know if you're thinking too small?

'Big' doesn't necessarily mean expensive or complex. Sometimes a phenomenal, business-changing idea is actually incredibly simple to implement.

'Big' means impactful. It means game-changing. When a big idea has succeeded, a company is clearly in a better position afterward.

Big ideas tend to come with risks and, as an executive it's your job to weigh those thoughtfully. Executives who are totally idea-driven without concern for a potential downside are ousted quickly. So dreaming big is also thinking smart.

Whenever an idea sparks, ask yourself these questions:

1 How does your idea move the company closer to its 5-year or 10-year vision?

2 Will it improve the company's financial position?

3 Will it improve the company's market position?

4 Does your idea involve one department or collaboration among departments?

5 Is a competitor already doing something similar?

If you don't get the resounding sense that your idea will have serious impact, consider that it may still be a good idea. Maybe even worthy of pursuit. But it's not a big idea, so you'll need to keep hunting for a bigger game to play at an Ultimate Executive level.

Dare Bigger

In previous roles you may have had to curb your boldness.

You may have tucked your biggest, loftiest ideas away because you didn't have the influence or resources to take them on.

Now that's changed.

As an executive, you're in the position to steward much bigger plans. Your voice is heard at top levels. People expect you to be innovative. And, if you give yourself permission, you now have the breathing room to be bold.

When I think of daring people, I think of Richard Branson. Sheryl Sandberg. Mark Zuckerberg. Shonda Rimes. These are people who are unafraid to implement ideas that raise eyebrows. They know when they've latched on to something beyond what others can currently perceive.

Daring big is having the nerve to not only have a wild idea, but also to then believe in yourself enough to say it aloud. You need to weigh critiques and concerns, and know when it's right to just keep moving ahead.

Dreaming is creativity. Daring is courage.

Ultimate Executives need to have both in equal measure to create a significant impact on the company.

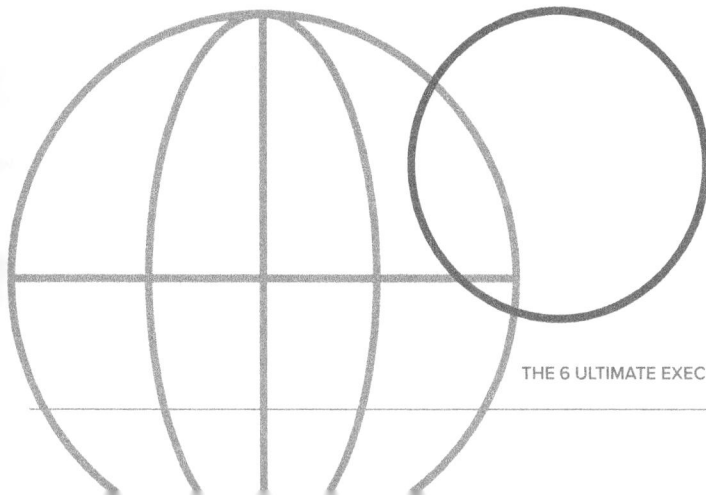

Planning for Greatness

I'm going to tell you where most brilliant ideas die: the planning stage.

This is when the adrenalin rush simmers down and the reality of budgets, resources and timelines kicks in. This is when negative thoughts show up in your mind to complain about how challenging the project will be.

An incredibly wise, successful executive once told me, 'A good plan today is better than a great plan tomorrow.' I urge you to live by this.

Planning is not about perfection. It's about creating a road map for getting from A to B, knowing there'll be pit stops and detours.

I've seen far, far too many great ideas fail because people get lost in their own planning processes. Due diligence is necessary and wise, but eventually you need to leap.

Here are my top 5 tips for corralling yourself so your project isn't killed by the planning sword:

1 **Set a completion date for your plan and stick to it.** Endless planning cycles kill enthusiasm and will.

2 **Use a planning template that you know and trust.** Don't recreate the wheel every time.

3 **Learn to be concise.** Longer plans are not better plans. Don't over-explain – it wastes precious time for you and everyone else.

4 **Ask for help.** Delegate pieces of the plan development such as getting cost estimates, sourcing potential partners or market research.

5 **Accept the unknown.** It will be impossible to mitigate all risk and to answer all questions. Know when to leap.

The Practical Side of Thinking Big

Please don't ever believe that the role of an executive is to merely 'think' and never 'do.'

Yes, your tasks may be radically different than previous roles. You will need to spend more time thinking and planning than doing. But if you never roll up your sleeves to make things happen, big dreams won't become a reality.

You can't always be in the sky creating new schemes or you will quickly lose your sense of practicality. You'll lose touch with the day-to-day operations of your company and the people in it. This is a fast road to failure.

As an executive, you need to be a doer. But you also need to be smart about how much time you personally spend on implementation and what tasks you assume.

As an example, it might not be in the company's best interest to have you placing every call to get the wheels in motion for your big idea. But it might fast-track the project if you personally place calls to strategic partners. You may need to be the spokesperson for your big idea, rallying support across the company.

With every task consider, 'Is this the most appropriate use of my time? If I take this on, do I accelerate or improve the project greatly?'

Needless to say, if you're in a smaller organization, you may need to spend more time on implementation. Even so, consider using contract employees, agencies and other third-party resources to outsource some of the work.

As long as your big ideas produce strong financial results, most of your time should be spent on creating and overseeing big ideas. But Ultimate Executives have their feet on the ground and aren't afraid to be part of the action.

Expansiveness

LEADING QUESTION

What stops me from thinking bigger?

Ownership

Ownership is the ultimate level of accountability. It means holding yourself fully responsible for the obligations you've assumed to the company and its employees. It also requires fostering responsibility in those you lead.

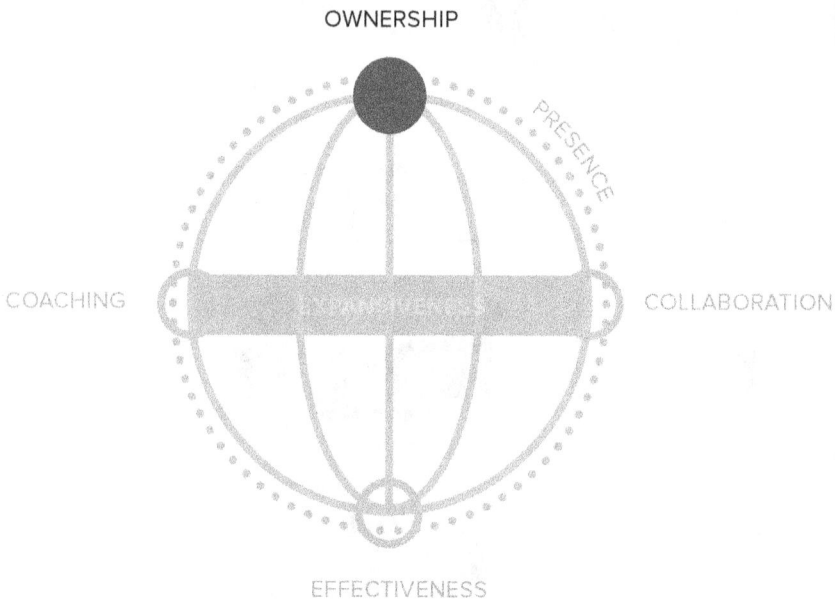

OWNERSHIP

PRESENCE

COACHING

COLLABORATION

EFFECTIVENESS

Perhaps at every other stage of your career it has been entirely appropriate (and at times completely necessary) to pass the buck.

This is no longer true. The buck now stops with you. For the Ultimate Executive there is only pure, unwavering accountability.

To do this, you need to embrace the idea that you are never a victim.

Things will go wrong. Failures will happen. Your role is to accept blame, learn lessons and go forward.

Taking **ownership** will sometimes mean accepting blame on behalf of your team, or other people who were involved in a misfire. Do this elegantly. Remember they were acting on your behalf, under your leadership.

If they have failed, your leadership has in some way failed. Perhaps you picked the wrong team. Perhaps you failed to offer the support and structure required for success.

And there it is. There's no shame in failure. There is, however, great inelegance in an executive who points fingers and plays the victim card. Being a victim is the direct opposite of being a leader.

The 4 components of ownership are:

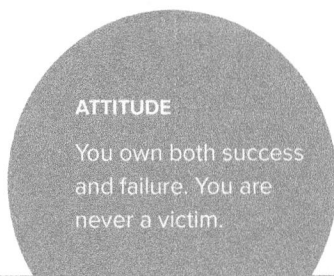

ATTITUDE
You own both success and failure. You are never a victim.

SYSTEMS	PEOPLE	CULTURE
Formal and informal systems to manage performance.	Strong communication and interpersonal connection and commitment.	Create a culture where it is normal for people to be accountable.

ATMOSPHERE OF
ACCOUNTABILITY

As an Ultimate Executive, it's your job to create an atmosphere in which everyone enthusiastically accepts responsibility for commitments. Your personal responsibility is not enough. It's your job to make accountability the norm across the company.

Ownership Starts with You

When things go wrong, you're responsible.

I know that sounds harsh but trust me, when you look at life this way you can take control. Rather than focusing on external factors that contribute to your problems, you can zero in on what you can actually change: you.

When you miss a goal, own it. Figure out what you need to do next time to get a better result and move forward.

Blaming will cause you to feel helpless and frustrated. People will see you as a victim or complainer.

If you notice that your mind is sometimes consumed by thoughts of what other people have done wrong or how they need to change, let this be a major warning bell to you.

This expenditure of mental energy will lead you nowhere.

Your CEO doesn't want to hear a list of complaints or how other people let you down. Remove these behaviors from your repertoire entirely.

You are a victor, not a victim. You are a problem-solver. You are honest enough to see your own failings.

Let me share a story from way-back-when. I used to be an executive at a prominent PR agency. I worked with an extremely charming, fiercely talented peer (let's call him Bill) who adamantly refused to accept responsibility for any shortfall.

Bill's errors were always someone else's fault. When he didn't meet his goals, there were a million reasons he wasn't responsible. He blamed his team for letting him down. He blamed his peers for not adequately supporting him. He blamed outside contributors who didn't deliver as planned.

I will tell you candidly he drove me mad. And I wasn't alone. My executive colleagues would take me aside frequently to vent their frustrations. Our CEO wore a pained expression whenever he had to interact with Bill.

Eventually, everyone's patience wore thin. Despite his many talents, he was gradually pulled from our most important accounts. He was no longer invited to collaborate on special initiatives. In essence, he was shut out. Yes, he retained his title, but he no longer functioned as a true executive.

The lesson in Bill's story is that people will respect you more when you muster the courage to simply say, 'My bad. I messed up. I'll fix it.'

Not doing so is weak-kneed. It will prevent you from operating at your highest potential.

Never be afraid to own your failures. These tough moments come with the territory of executive leadership. They can make you stronger and smarter if you handle them with grace and self-awareness.

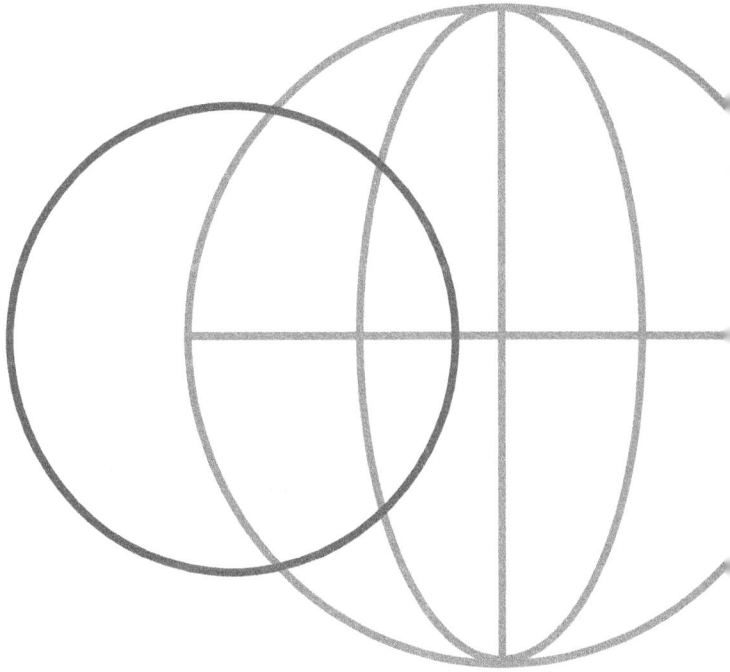

Can Your Colleagues Count on You?

If you haven't already, let go of any attachment to being accountable only to yourself.

Playing at the executive level means you need to be accountable to your colleagues. It's wise to view other executives as allies rather than competitors. It's wise to set up a framework that allows for mutual accountability.

I beseech you, never make the mistake of keeping your cards too close to your chest when it comes to your colleagues. This has been the downfall of many would-be Ultimate Executives.

You have to be open, accepting and forthright to build trust. As you foster deeper trust with peers at the senior levels of your company, you'll find they are more accountable to you and your initiatives. The more trust you build, the more equity you have at an executive level.

That trust has to go both ways of course. Hold yourself accountable to support their pursuits where you can. Your colleagues need to know they can count on you.

Your success in executive leadership is defined by team results and corporate results. It's not about your individual performance anymore. You're no longer a lone wolf.

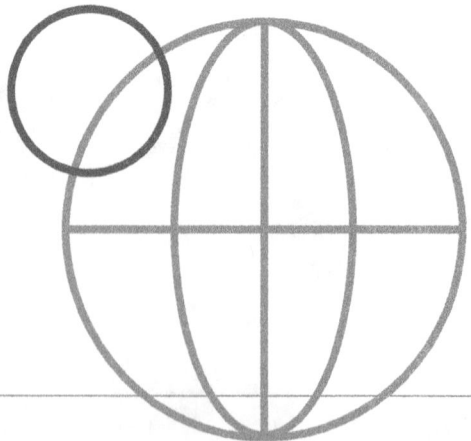

Establish an Atmosphere of Accountability

Every company needs accountability woven into the fabric of its culture. You can still have a lively, creative, warm atmosphere with high standards of performance and personal ownership. So be intentional about this.

Find out how accountable your atmosphere is with these 5 questions:

1 Do people routinely miss deadlines?

2 Do projects fall by the wayside, never to be resurrected?

3 Do people tend to blame others when things go wrong?

4 Are people competitive with each other rather than supportive?

5 Are people reluctant to take on new initiatives?

If you answered 'yes' even once, your company is less than fully accountable.

If you've created an atmosphere of accountability, it's in the air you breathe. It's rare that someone dumps a monkey on your desk. People are excited to take on new initiatives and willingly jump in to help someone that needs support.

People own their deadlines and missteps. They hold you and other leaders to your word.

Leadership is about rallying people to perform at their highest level. They're only as good as the environment you create for them.

Structure is Beautiful

When it comes to Ultimate Executive leadership, structure is beautiful. Don't fear it.

It's your job to ensure you have solid systems in place to manage performance and hold people to their commitments.

But don't think of structure as some sort of penalty system. It should be a system of celebration and reward above all else.

Structure provides the nuts and bolts that hold your culture together. So carefully think through the formal aspects of your performance management structure as well as the informal elements.

If you're creating a fun, high-energy culture (for example), you need a reward system in place that matches that tone.

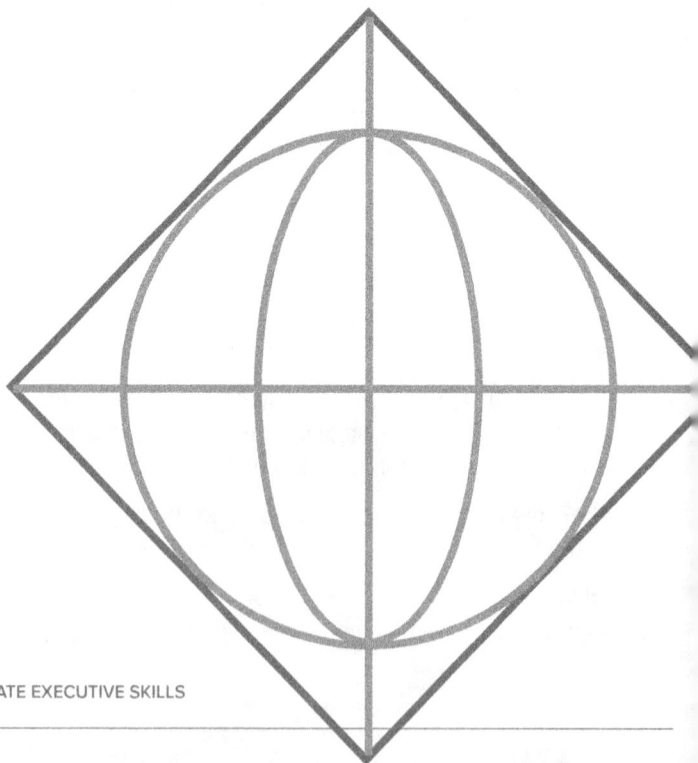

How rigorous is your current structure? Ask yourself:

1 Does everyone on your team know what metrics define their individual success? Bonus points if they all know right now where they stand on your performance scale.

2 Do you also measure and reward based on team performance?

3 Do you have clearly defined systems for celebrating individual and team success?

4 Do you check in with people regularly?

5 Does your system for celebration and reward match the culture you want to create?

If you can confidently answer 'yes' to all of these questions, kudos. Performance management is your bag. Now your job is to keep the system flowing.

On the other hand, if your employees have only a vague idea what metrics you're seeking, or you haven't had a team celebration in more than a quarter, you need to step up your game.

If people on your team are shocked to see you in the hallways or speak to you one-on-one, it's time to raise your own commitment to communication.

Ownership structures apply to you and everyone on your team. Without them, successes will be ad hoc and unpredictable. With them, you're positioned to deliver consistently exceptional results.

Ownership

LEADING QUESTION

When did I last accept a short-coming?

Collaboration

At its very core, **collaboration** is sharing. It's having the mentality that the company will perform better when everyone readily shares knowledge and resources.

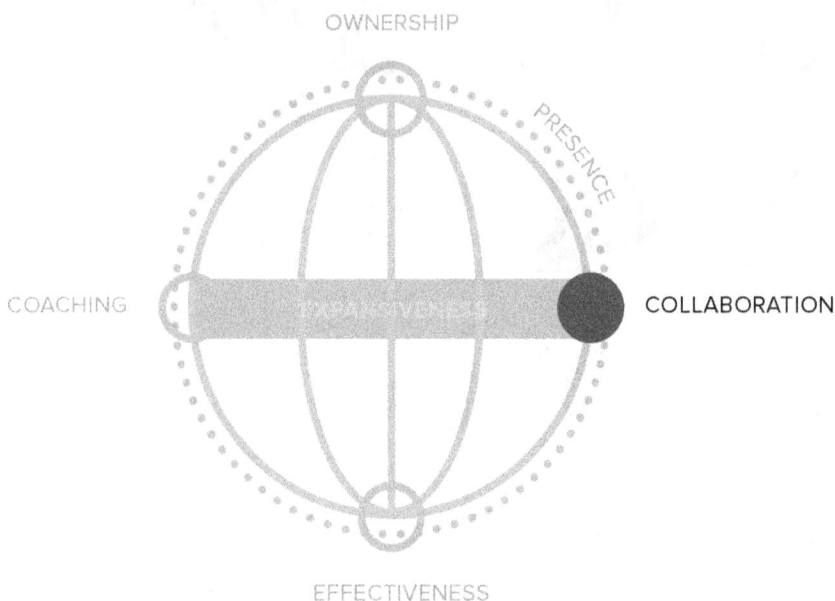

Ultimate Executives set a tone of **collaboration**, never placing personal glory or power ahead of the organization's success. They're quick to share the credit for wins and accept due responsibility for losses.

To the greatest extent possible, they take ego out of the equation, doing whatever it takes to move the business forward.

Companies with **collaborative** cultures have the competitive advantage of being quick and agile. They can capture new market opportunities and see potential risks well ahead of the pack.

On the other hand, companies that operate in silos with individuals hoarding information lose crucial time. Leaders and employees compete with each other, losing sight of the far more crucial market competition.

Team friction ends up being a more deadly foe than outside competitors.

So, what does it take for you to personally set a tone of collaboration? You need to be known as:

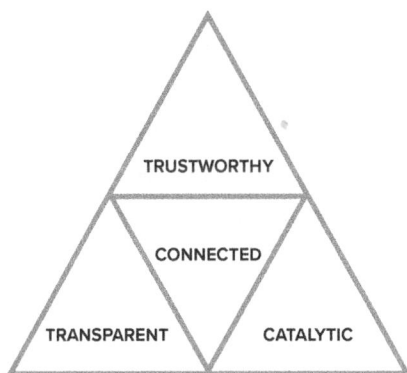

Connected: It's your job to connect the dots at the highest level, finding opportunity for collaboration where others may not see it. Your role is to connect people, projects and ideas and to ensure activities are directly connected to the company's long-term vision.

Trustworthy: Live up to your word. Make commitments carefully and take each one seriously. People will judge your integrity based on your ability to deliver on even the simplest promises.

Transparent: Don't use information or resources to wield power over your colleagues. Don't play games with people. Share willingly. Ultimately, information and resources aren't yours. They belong to the company.

Catalytic: Collaboration is most likely to happen when you are proactively working to bring people, projects and ideas together. It's not enough to just see the potential for collaboration. Act as a catalyst, helping to remove barriers and facilitate camaraderie.

Your willingness to share with others and spark true collaboration will contribute greatly to the impact you make as an Ultimate Executive.

Collaboration Reality-Check

I want you to ask yourself, 'How collaborative am I, *really?'*

Competition is so ingrained that it can be hard to let it go even with your colleagues. This isn't surprising. Your competitive spirit is part of the reason you've arrived at the executive level to begin with.

But it has its time and place. To be an Ultimate Executive, you need to know when to keep your competitiveness in check and let a collaborative perspective take over.

Think about how you interact with people inside your company. On average, are you more collaborative or more competitive with others?

Read the following statements. How true is each one for you?

1 Given my level of responsibility and performance, I deserve a lot of the credit when I'm involved in a big win.

2 When things go wrong, it's important for me to communicate where others fell short.

3 I sometimes make promises I don't intend to keep.

4 I'm sometimes reluctant to share information.

5 I'm sometimes reluctant to share resources.

6 I think cross-team collaboration can be more trouble than it's worth.

7 I prefer to focus on the success of my own team and let others win or lose on their own terms.

If any of these statements feel even just a bit true for you, there's probably more beneath the surface. You don't need to dampen your competitive spirit, you just need to use it strategically.

Your ability to impact the company's bottom line will grow exponentially when you start viewing yourself as a captain of the greater team, not just your direct reports.

As you adopt this position more, you'll be able to tune into new opportunities for cross-pollination, feeding innovation and market agility.

Creating a Collaborative Culture

When you're at the top rung of leadership, you need to move beyond just a personal commitment to collaboration.

Your role is now to contribute to the creation of a collaborative culture, where everyone is responsible for sharing knowledge and resources.

A collaborative culture is defined by the following 5 characteristics:

1 People don't see information or resources as personal possessions. Instead, they willingly (and enthusiastically) share them broadly.

2 Disputes are resolved based on the best interests of the company, not on who wields the most power or makes the best argument.

3 Contributions are valued based on merit.

4 Decision-making is transparent.

5 Collaboration is rewarded. There are systems in place to foster and incentivize cross-team pollination.

Even if your current corporate culture is notably un-collaborative, you're in the position to shift it. It begins with you adopting these 5 characteristics with your direct team and modeling these behaviors within your company.

Of course, you can't create a collaborative culture alone. But you can pave the way.

Building Trust

You can't inspire and lead collaborative efforts without one fundamental requirement: trust.

Do people believe you'll do what you say you will?

Here's the reality of many corporate cultures. People are in a meeting, mostly agreeing on a stated direction. Discussion takes place. Commitments are made. People leave the room. Some of what was discussed happens easily. Other stuff transpires that is at direct odds with what people agreed to. In some cases, people drop the ball entirely. In the end, the collaborative effort is an exercise in frustration and disappointment.

This scenario may sound harsh, but if you're honest with yourself, I think it's likely you've experienced this all too often in your work life.

I believe there are two core causes of this less than trustworthy behavior. One is that people find it more efficient and less scary to simply agree in meetings rather than facing conflict. And second, I think the chaos of life and business take over and people have trouble living up to all the commitments they make, even though they had good intentions.

As an executive, you need to be comfortable facing conflict with grace and compassion. Far better that you state your objections up front and let people know what you can reasonably commit to, than to let people down. If you walk out of a meeting with people silently questioning your ability to fulfill on promises, your influence as a leader is severely limited.

An essential part of being an Ultimate Executive is quickly assessing what's viable for you personally and for the team. If you need to renege on a commitment, it's crucial that you communicate why and what your new promise is. But don't make a habit of redefining commitments, because it will diminish your credibility.

The delicate balance here is that to excel as an executive leader, you need to be brave and thoroughly grounded in reality at exactly the same time.

Without bravery, you won't inspire excellence. Without a firm grip on reality, you won't inspire trust.

Making the Tough Calls

The hard thing about creating a collaborative culture is that one bad seed will ruin the crop.

Your job is to eliminate the bad seeds.

It's not enough that the majority of people on your executive team or employee roster are willing collaborators. Just one person who's possessive of information or competitive with the others will influence your culture.

I've seen it happen all too often. Someone is hired because of a world-class resume, and the leadership team chooses not to notice an abrasive or egotistical attitude. Everyone silently hopes this person will fit in, bringing talents to bear without causing friction.

Moments like this are a test of your mettle. Do you let someone poison your culture? Are you truly committed to collaboration, or do you waver for the sake of a quick win?

My client, Cheyenne, faced this dilemma last year. She hired a hotshot (who we'll call Steve) to run her marketing department, wowed by his glowing recommendations.

The very day he started, a sick feeling emerged in Cheyenne's stomach. She'd made a dreadful misjudgment.

Steve was a showboat in the worst possible way. He held frequent brainstorming meetings that felt more like 'Steve: A One-Man Show.' He talked endlessly about his own ideas and past successes. When someone dared to speak, he dismissed their ideas instantly.

This behavior ruffled more than a few feathers in Cheyenne's highly-collaborative, tight-knit company. She'd built an atmosphere of respect, and Steve stood out like a Martian.

When she attempted to coach him on working more collaboratively, he was floored. After all, he included so many people in his 'brainstorming meetings'.

After only a few weeks, Cheyenne had to send Steve packing. He was talented beyond belief, but he was not a team player.

If having a collaborative culture is truly your aim, you'll have to make some tough calls too. You'll have to identify loose cannons and be the brave voice that coaches them on changing their ways.

If change doesn't happen, you'll need to cut ties with talented people who refuse to fit in. Ultimate Executives understand that 'fit' is about more than just a history of performance. It's about finding and retaining people who blend with your desired corporate culture.

This is why it's vital to assess new hires for culture fit, not just knowledge and skills. Your interview process needs to formally address this. It's not enough to assume someone who says they're a team player actually is. You need to dig deeper, do some testing, and ask head-on when you're reference-checking.

Collaborative cultures don't happen by accident. They're created through intention and action.

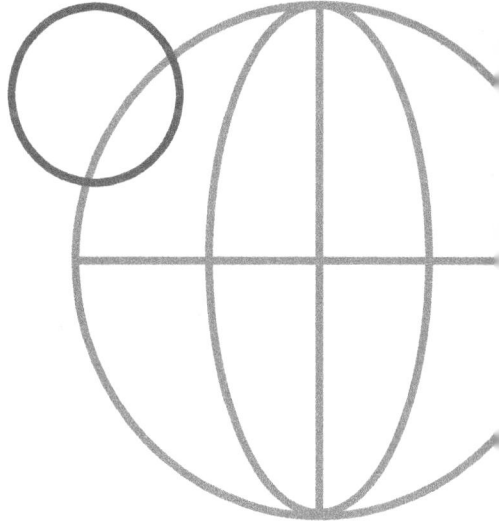

Collaboration

LEADING QUESTION

Is my ego in the way of more collaboration?

Effectiveness

Let's talk about elite-level **effectiveness.**
Ultimate Executives deliver at a capacity
significantly higher than ordinary mortals.

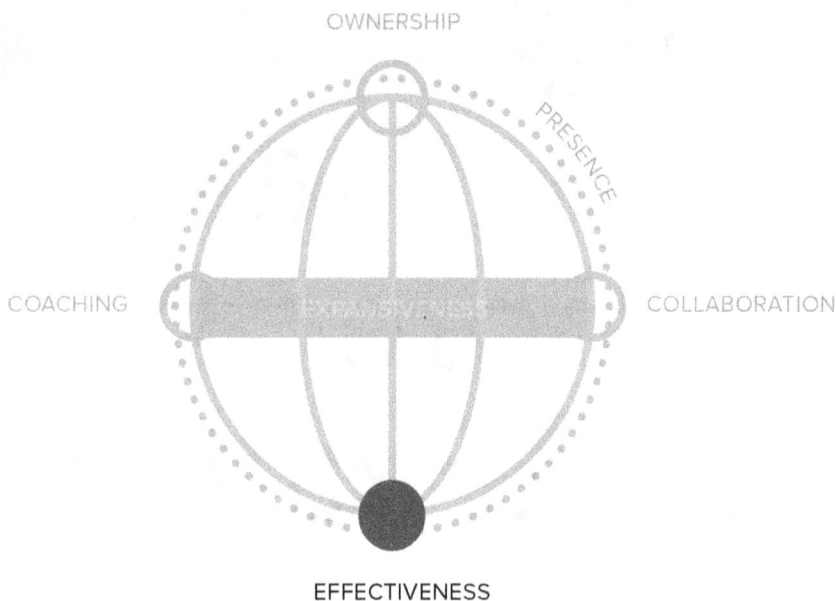

OWNERSHIP

PRESENCE

COACHING

EXPANSIVENESS

COLLABORATION

EFFECTIVENESS

At this level of performance, **effectiveness** is defined as maximizing your
contribution to the company's financial and market success. It's your ability
to meet sizable goals while dancing with time and evolving priorities.

Of course there are major hurdles in the path to executive **effectiveness.**
You're mandated with hefty commitments, and then, as if this wasn't enough,
life tosses daily curve balls demanding your time and attention.

Team members quit and encounter personal challenges. New opportunities
arise from left field, beckoning you. Someone else's team hits the skids and
you're asked to step in. On and on it goes.

There are 4 elements to Ultimate Executive effectiveness:

DIAGNOSTIC THINKING

The ability to stay rational and insightful, rather than having a reactive response to whatever comes your way.

ENERGY MANAGEMENT

The ability to expend your energy efficiently and effectively.

VALUE RECOGNITION

The ability to tune in to the most impactful way to invest your time at any given moment.

TIME INTELLIGENCE

The ability to see time as a strategic tool rather than an obstacle or finite resource to be strictly scheduled.

The demands of your role far exceed the benefits of time management skills. As an Ultimate Executive, you need this advanced set of tools to deliver elite **effectiveness** without running yourself into the ground.

Dancing with Time

Gone are the days when managing time was as simple as following a to-do list.

As an executive, strict list-making and time-scheduling are not your friends. In fact, I would argue they are enemies of productivity.

Ultimate Executives have time intelligence. They understand how to flow through their day, always recognizing the most valuable way to invest their time at any given moment.

As situations arise, they quickly diagnose if it's appropriate to reprioritize and shift their attention – or, if it's best to stay the course.

Dancing with time requires a calm, clear head so you can absorb new information quickly and make smart assessments.

It also requires perspective. You need to weigh not just the immediate situation, but also knowledge from the past and the long-term priorities of the company.

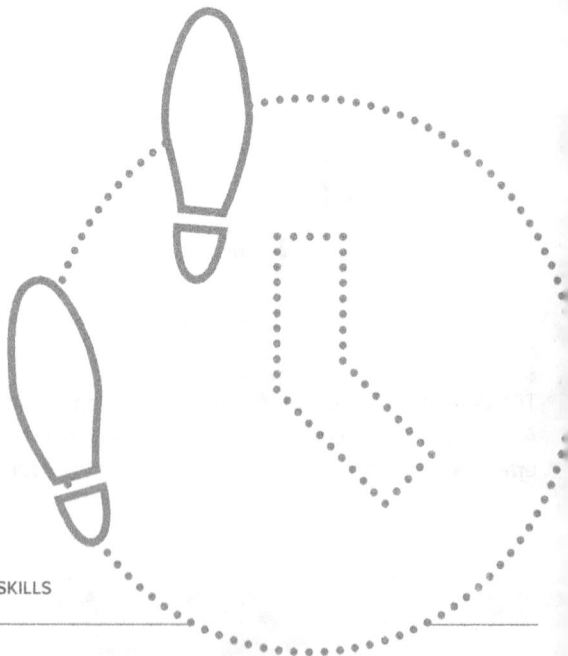

To have time intelligence, you must:

> **Know working harder isn't necessarily more productive.** The mind operates more efficiently when you take breaks frequently and give it room to be calm.

> **Always evaluate if you are the right person to take on a task.** Don't assume responsibility without knowing why you're the right person for the job and how it is valuable to the big picture.

> **Be comfortable flowing from one role to the next.** You may be a project lead in one moment, a product visionary in the next, and a gracious host for a client dinner later the same day.

> **Be available for new priorities.** Don't shut yourself off from the world to focus exclusively on known opportunities. Let people visit unannounced sometimes. Allow for spontaneity in your day.

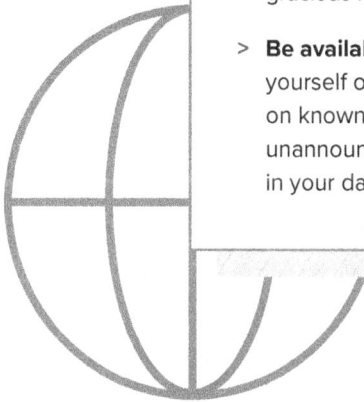

Time intelligence has everything to do with patience and fluidity. Everyone you encounter will have their own unique rhythm with time and your ability to tune into it will greatly improve your ability to get things done.

It may take practice for you to get comfortable dancing with time, but as you do, you'll find your day has more flow and far greater efficiency.

The Value Equation

How adept are you at choosing how to invest your time?

Return on effort (ROE) is a simple equation that ensures you're allotting your time and energy to get the biggest bang possible. It's about focusing on the most valuable task at any given time.

Here's the formula:

$$ROE = \frac{\textbf{Task} \text{ (Energy + Skill + Priority)}}{\textbf{Time} \text{ (\# hours to complete task)}}$$

Let's break it down.

You are of most value to your company if you focus on tasks that feed your energy, propelling you ever forward. With every task you must consider, will it give you energy or drain it? If it gives you energy, it's a high-energy task.

Next you must consider, are you truly the right person to do the task? Is it the best use of your talents? For example, you may have mad PowerPoint skills, but so do 10 other people on your team. Personally designing a presentation wouldn't be the best use of your time. It wouldn't be a high-skill task.

A high-priority task means there's a darn good reason you're doing a task right now. It is in alignment with your project timelines.

A task has high ROE if it's high energy, high skill and high priority.

If a task fails to meet the grade in all three areas, you have some thinking to do before you personally take it on.

If it's low in all areas – no brainer. Delegate it or postpone it until it becomes higher priority.

If it's a low-energy and/or a low-skill task, it's another no-brainer. Delegate. There's sure to be someone on your team (or someone you can contract) who is more appropriate to take it on.

If a task is low-priority, but high in the other two areas, schedule it for a time when you can really sink into it and enjoy it. It shouldn't be first on your list if there are high priority items awaiting your attention.

I think you get the gist of the formula now. There are subtleties, of course. Some things will be a medium priority or a medium-skill level. You'll need to use your judgment to weigh the investment of your time based on the tasks at hand.

ROE is about using your personal time and your team effectively. At the end of the day, it's about knowing when a task is yours to do and when it's best to pass it down the line.

$$ROE = \frac{Task\ (Energy + Skill + Priority)}{Time\ (\#\ hours\ to\ complete\ task)}$$

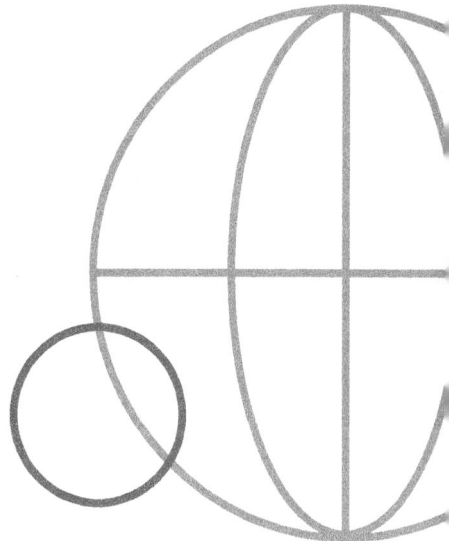

Good Busy vs. Bad Busy

Spending time on things that suck your energy dry leads to what I like to call 'bad busy.'

It's the kind of busy that makes you wake up dreading the day ahead, wishing for an escape route to a different job.

This kind of busy typically arises in one of two ways. One, you spend a lot of time in reactive mode, investing time on the latest curveball to fly your way. Or, you spend too much time on activities that aren't in your zone, focusing instead on tasks that drain your life-force energy.

It's possible you're doing both of these things, in which case you're a four-alarm blaze headed to fast and total burnout.

'Good busy' on the other hand, is a lovely state of being. You end the day feeling energized even though you've put in the same hours as bad-busy people.

And get this – you achieve more. Your productivity is exponentially higher because you're not forcing your reluctant mind and body through undesirable tasks. You are working in areas where your highest value can be achieved.

To be good busy, you need to become acutely aware of what gives you energy and what depletes it. Then you need to spend at least 80% of your day on activities that give you energy. Delegate or outsource the rest.

Everyone will be better for it. The stuff that sucks your energy will be a sweet spot for someone else.

Do you expend energy wisely? Here are 7 questions to ask yourself:

1 Do you have a sense of dread about going to work?

2 Is it common for you to feel frustration or annoyance at work?

3 Do you spend less than 80% of your day doing tasks you genuinely enjoy?

4 At the end of the day, do you shudder at the thought of doing it all again tomorrow?

5 Do you spend more time on other people's priorities rather than your own?

6 Is your experience of life less fulfilling than you would like it to be?

7 Are you less optimistic about life than you used to be?

If you answered 'yes' to any of these questions, you're likely in the 'bad busy' zone. I urge you to evaluate how you spend your time to maximize your effectiveness and personal satisfaction.

If you responded 'no' to every question, you understand how to be 'good busy.' Your mission is to stay in this zone. It's easy to slip up by shifting to reactive mode or assuming tasks that are better left for others. Resist those urges.

Top 6 Effectiveness Killers

To operate at your best at an executive level, you'll likely need to break some old habits.

Here are the top 6 effectiveness killers along with 6 unbelievably simple solutions:

1 **Checking email obsessively.** We have people like Steve Jobs to thank for both the joy and nightmare of mobile technology. The nightmare is that ever-connectedness easily leads to email addiction, pulling your energy and attention away from more vital work.

   Unbelievably Simple Solution: Close your email application while you're working. Check it once every hour or two ... then close it again. I promise you, the world will not end.

2 **Task avoidance.** When a challenging or unpleasant task is on your priority list, you waste time surfing the web, having unimportant conversations, making tea ... anything to delay.

   Unbelievably Simple Solution: Move on to something else productive. Inevitably, you will muster the energy for the unwanted task later or (if appropriate) find an opportunity to delegate it. Don't let it defeat you by halting all productivity.

3 **Disorganized workspace.** It's far more difficult to be effective when you're working amidst chaos. It's impossible to have a clear mind.

   Unbelievably Simple Solution: Seek help from an organizational wizard. Maybe it's your assistant or someone else on your team. Maybe you need to contract an expert. Get someone who loves organization to create a system for you and teach you to use it. You may need a monthly or quarterly visit from them to keep yourself in check.

4 **The inability to say 'no.'** It's not your job to solve everyone else's problems or take on every task that comes your way.

Unbelievably Simple Solution: There's no way around this one. You need to learn to say 'no.' Start by learning to say, 'I hear what you're saying, let me get back to you about this when I've had some time to think it through.'

5 **Multi-tasking.** Multi-tasking is evil. It feels productive because you're highly occupied but it's really a time-waster. Nothing gets done as efficiently or as well as it would if you focused on one thing at a time.

Unbelievably Simple Solution: Focus on one thing for at least 45 minutes to an hour at a time (or less if it's complete sooner). Every initiative deserves 100% of your attention some of the time.

6 **Firefighting:** The quickest solution to a problem is not necessarily the best solution. Jumping to conclusions and rushing to action will lead you down a rabbit hole.

Unbelievably Simple Solution: Take a moment to breathe. Instead of rushing to the nearest solution, take the time to properly diagnose the situation. Don't let people hurry or pressure you. Give yourself the time to assess the urgency of the situation. Find the smartest solution rather than the fastest.

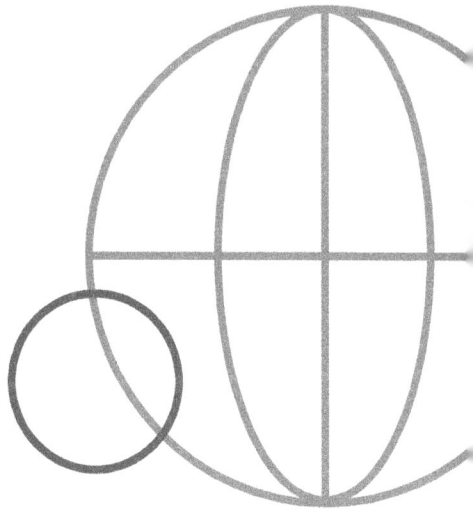

Effectiveness

LEADING QUESTION

What habit is most limiting my productivity?

Coaching

As an executive, you're measured on your **coaching** ability that leads people to deliver results.

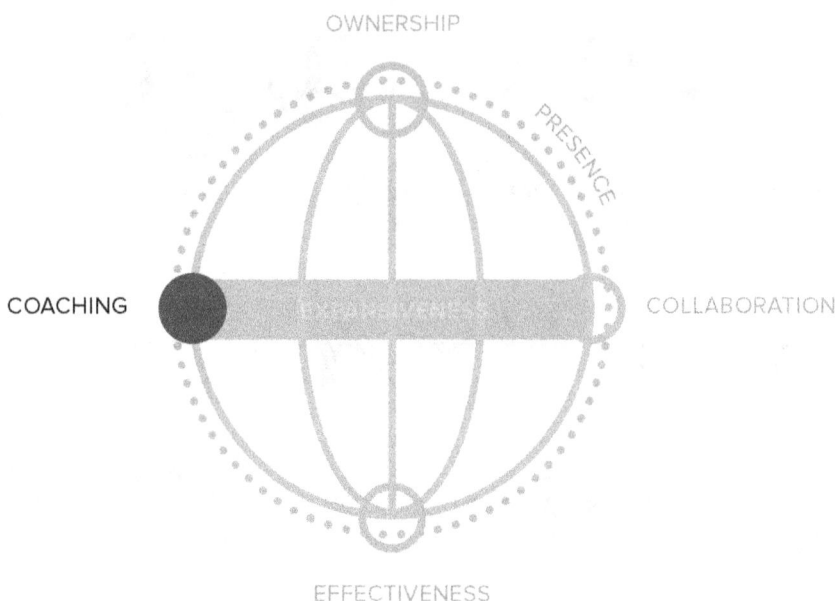

Coaching is a more sophisticated, impactful style of leadership that leads to bigger payoffs. It's about helping people gain self-awareness so they can make better decisions and expand their own abilities to perform and lead.

Coaching-style leadership has been shown to improve business results by 21% (source: Bersin & Associates).

Traditional management, on the other hand, is more of a command-and-control approach that essentially involves telling people what to do. This can lead to decent team performance, but it's inherently limited. At best you'll inspire compliance, but rarely passionate commitment. Because of this, your team won't reach its greatest potential.

Coaching is mostly about being a keen observer and intent listener. It's about asking smart questions that lead people to discover insight within themselves.

A coaching relationship follows these ABC's:

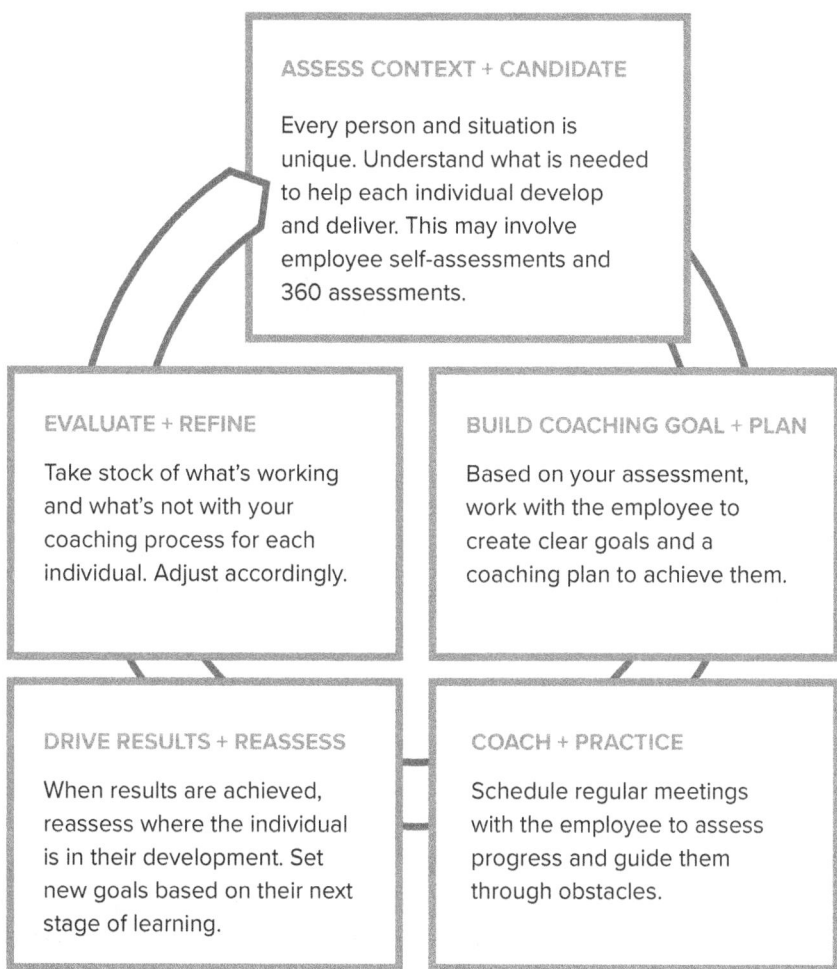

ASSESS CONTEXT + CANDIDATE

Every person and situation is unique. Understand what is needed to help each individual develop and deliver. This may involve employee self-assessments and 360 assessments.

EVALUATE + REFINE

Take stock of what's working and what's not with your coaching process for each individual. Adjust accordingly.

BUILD COACHING GOAL + PLAN

Based on your assessment, work with the employee to create clear goals and a coaching plan to achieve them.

DRIVE RESULTS + REASSESS

When results are achieved, reassess where the individual is in their development. Set new goals based on their next stage of learning.

COACH + PRACTICE

Schedule regular meetings with the employee to assess progress and guide them through obstacles.

Being an Ultimate Executive means you have the opportunity to not only use coaching skills, but also to transfer them to your direct reports. You can help create a coaching-culture across your organization, optimizing performance at all levels.

Coaching vs. Everything Else

Understanding coaching starts with knowing what it's not.

In the business world, terms like 'mentoring,' 'teaching' and 'counseling' are often used interchangeably with 'coaching.'

This is a grand misunderstanding that causes confusion about what coaching actually is. It's also a personal pet peeve. But I digress.

When you coach someone, your mission is to help that person gain self-awareness. You help people arrive at smart conclusions on their own and resolve their own problems.

Coaching is about the here and now: what does this person want to accomplish? What's in the way?

Teaching, on the other hand, is helping someone develop a specific skill or capability. You can teach someone, for example, how to program in HTML or conduct a financial audit.

Mentoring is when you share your own wealth of experience to shape how someone sees the world and their opportunities in it. It's allowing someone to draw on your knowledge as they face decisions in their own life.

And lastly, counseling is a term that most accurately applies to people with specialized training. It focuses on improving current situations by examining and resolving issues from the past – often from childhood.

Teaching, mentoring and counseling each have their merits and rightful places. It's not my intention to dissuade you from using these approaches if and when it's appropriate.

But to be the most effective leader you can be, use coaching as your primary approach. You'll get better results and a more motivated, committed team. And you'll create a lineup of people who are prepared for higher levels of leadership.

Coaches create working environments that are supportive while holding people accountable for their commitments. They offer feedback and feedforward rather than to-do lists.

To take a coach-approach you'll need to:

> **Excel as a communicator:** Take an 'ask' vs. 'tell' approach. Make sure feedback is understood.

> **Be consistent:** Have a coaching plan for each of your direct reports and regular coaching meetings.

> **Be available:** Sometimes coaching needs to happen spontaneously as issues and opportunities arise. You can't be in an ivory tower.

> **Guide conversations.** Refrain from monologues: Coaching isn't about you and your wisdom. It's about helping others tune into their own wisdom.

> **Focus on people.** Not projects. Executives that focus on developing people will be far more successful than those who emphasize tasks and projects.

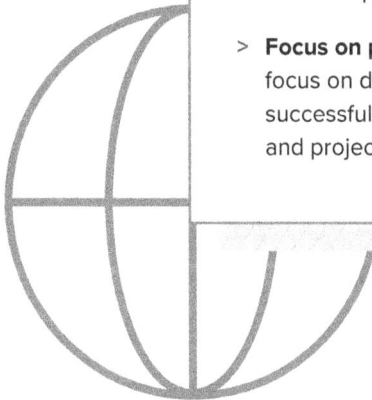

No Longer Rockin' It Old-School

A fundamental law of coaching is to focus on managing people and performance, not projects and tasks. Welcome to the polar opposite of old-school micromanagement.

If you've ever found yourself the overseer of a massive, multi-colored spreadsheet itemizing other people's tasks ... gently admit to yourself you have some micromanagement leanings.

But of course, management is a spectrum. You may have some tendencies toward coaching and some toward nit-picking. It's ok – leadership is a journey.

To master coach-style leadership, you'll need to let go of telling people how to do their jobs, despite your deep expertise.

So, how does your current management style compare to coaching?

Ask yourself these questions:

1 Do you allow people to take full responsibility for their own decisions and actions?

2 Do you allow people to take risks you might not take?

3 Do you regularly allow people to implement their own creative ideas?

4 Would your team say they're allowed to challenge you?

5 Would they say their voices are heard?

6 Would they say you treat mistakes as learning opportunities?

7 Do they feel recognized and honored for what they achieve?

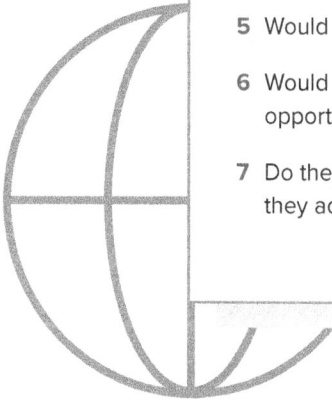

If you answered 'yes' to all of these questions, you've conquered any desire to lead by telling and you're allowing people the freedom to grow. Consider making it your goal to formalize the way you coach your team by implementing individual coaching plans.

If you answered 'no' to any of these, fear not. Remember, the shift to coaching is empowering for you, not just your team. It will allow you to operate at a more strategic level and to develop even more rewarding relationships. Make it your mission to free yourself from the chains of old-school management.

Act Like a Coach

Being a coach has everything to do with stellar communication.

It starts by meeting someone where they are, and not speaking to them as though they should know more than they do. Non-judgmental language is crucial to coach-style leadership.

From there, coaching is about asking the right questions. Many executives lean toward a pointed-style of questioning that can be intimidating.

Questions like, 'Didn't you say this would be done last week?' or 'Why did you do it that way?' quickly put people on the defensive. Instead of learning, your employees will be plotting a fast escape from the conversation.

Conversely, coaches ask non-blaming, open-ended questions, even when they're frustrated. They take emotion out of the equation and guide a calm, clear conversation.

Coaching questions sound like:

> What's the status on your project?

> Can you talk me through how you arrived at this decision?

> What might you do differently next time?

> What support do you need from me to meet this deadline?

Tone of voice weighs heavily into coaching. An accusatory or annoyed tone will ruin the most beautifully worded question. So process your emotions before or after conversations with employees, not during.

Benefit from a Coaching Culture

I want you to imagine a company where people have keen self-awareness and the unshakable ability to solve their own problems.

Results are through the roof. Creativity is an everyday occurrence and people have no problem taking full accountability for their decisions.

In this magical corporation, people work together – not by demanding or directing – but by helping each individual rise to their highest potential.

People are unafraid to say what needs to be said. Each individual is both a leader and collaborator in his or her own right.

Where is this mystical land, you ask? I shall tell you.

This is your current organization infused with a coaching-culture.

Now, I don't mean to suggest coaching creates utopia. But it definitely creates organizations that outperform those that are stuck in traditional forms of management.

In a coaching culture, every person at every level of the organization has coaching skills. Because of this, communication flows easily and problems are quickly resolved. People are empowered and respected, making them more committed to their mandates.

All of this contributes to better bottom-line results.

A coaching culture can begin with you developing coaching skills and using them with your team. Your team members will then, almost by osmosis, develop their own coaching abilities.

And so it goes. As other teams across your organization experience your approach and see the results, the coaching culture will spread.

But it takes at least one leader willing to invest in a people-focused management approach and a diligent coaching style.

Why not you?

Coaching

LEADING QUESTION

Do I ask questions that bring out the best in people?

Presence

Being an Ultimate Executive requires presence.

Presence is the 'X Factor' of the business world. It means you leave a lasting impression and inspire a sense of trust in people who work with you. When you're around, people believe in their own potential for greatness.

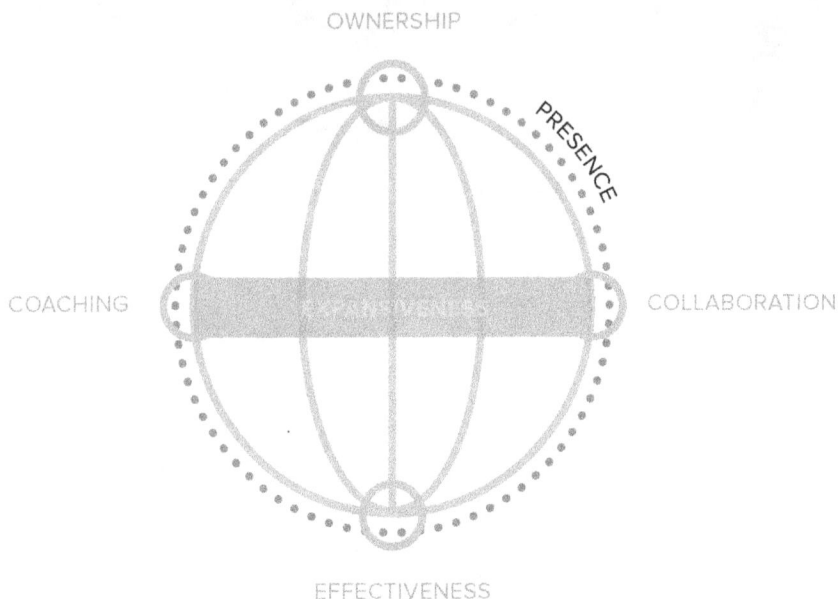

OWNERSHIP

PRESENCE

COACHING

EXPANSIVENESS

COLLABORATION

EFFECTIVENESS

Presence means you've got it all together. You exude credibility and confidence. You can hold your own with the top guns, fitting in comfortably with influential people. Leaders know you can assume great responsibility and manage well when crisis hits.

It's not a superficial attribute. **Presence** is not about flashiness or a big personality. In fact, anyone can develop it and remain authentic to their true nature. You don't need to be extroverted, charismatic or a barrel of laughs.

Presence is comprised of 5 essential elements:

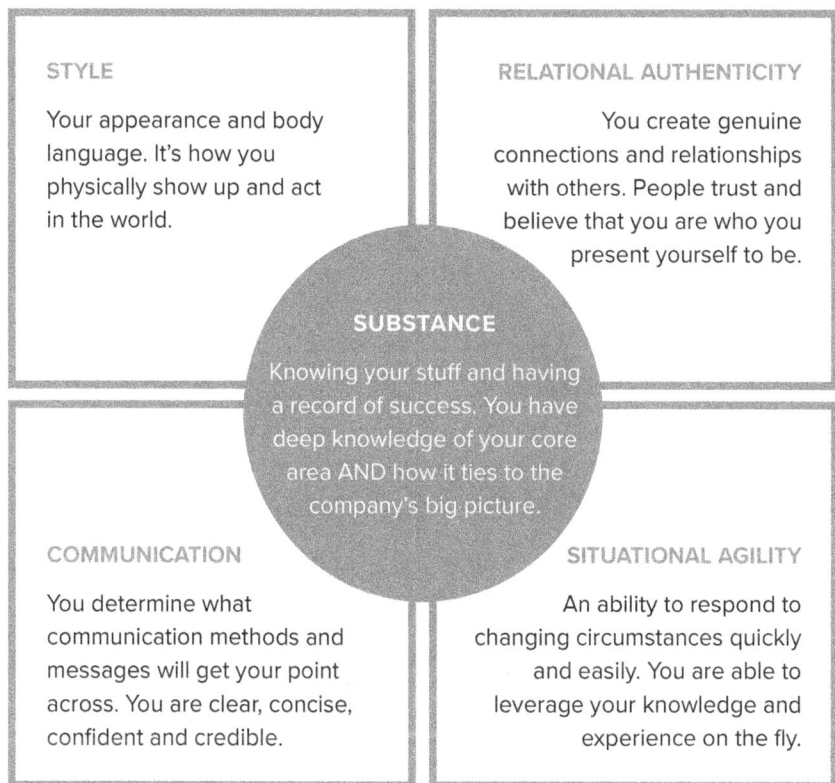

STYLE

Your appearance and body language. It's how you physically show up and act in the world.

RELATIONAL AUTHENTICITY

You create genuine connections and relationships with others. People trust and believe that you are who you present yourself to be.

SUBSTANCE

Knowing your stuff and having a record of success. You have deep knowledge of your core area AND how it ties to the company's big picture.

COMMUNICATION

You determine what communication methods and messages will get your point across. You are clear, concise, confident and credible.

SITUATIONAL AGILITY

An ability to respond to changing circumstances quickly and easily. You are able to leverage your knowledge and experience on the fly.

Even if you have authenticity, style, self-confidence and situational agility, you'll still never have true presence without substance.

So never let your focus on the other 4 elements divert your attention from ever-deepening your expertise. It's the hallmark of the Ultimate Executive.

The X Factor: Do You Have It?

You need a certain X Factor to excel at the highest levels of business.

How true is each for you?

1 If I asked 10 random people around my office, they would say they genuinely enjoy working with me.

2 If I asked 10 random people around my office, they would say they respect me.

3 When challenged, I stand my ground without becoming emotional or frustrated.

4 After speaking events or meetings, people make a point of coming over to talk to me, offering praise and support.

5 I don't need to work hard to get people to support my projects or collaborate with me. They do so enthusiastically.

6 When I come up with a big idea, I get the buy-in from the executive team quickly and easily.

7 People from other departments often seek my advice and opinion on things.

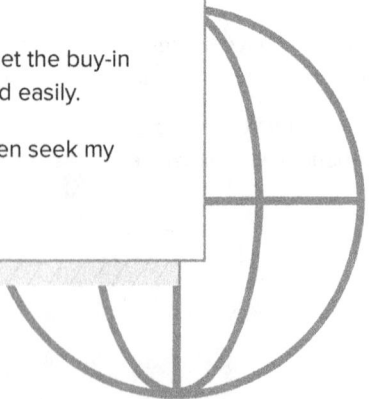

If 6 or 7 of these statements feel very true for you, you've got the X Factor and it's working for you in spades. You can continue to develop it and the rewards will be even greater.

If 5 or fewer of these statements are true, remember that presence can be acquired. You don't need to be born with it, and in fact most people aren't.

You don't need to change your personality to gain presence - you need to work on substance, style, communication, relational authenticity and situational agility.

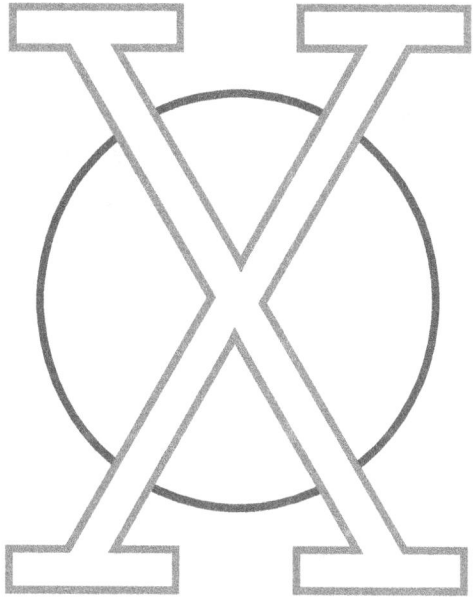

Presence vs. Obnoxiousness

Allow me to share some cautionary advice on presence because it can be treacherous territory.

Sometimes people think they have presence when in fact, they are exuding something else entirely: obnoxiousness.

Now don't stop reading. I know you think this isn't you.

But obnoxiousness is a spectrum and sometimes it can appear in small or medium-sized doses that are totally invisible to you ... but loud and clear to others.

No one wants to believe they are obnoxious. And because of this, few people examine their behavior carefully for these tendencies.

Years ago, I had a client who saw herself as a born leader. She commandeered every meeting she attended, calling attention to herself in every way possible.

She believed she was entertaining and insightful. But her humor and 'helpful advice,' were often off-pitch, leaving people feeling uneasy and annoyed.

I guided her to view herself through other people's eyes. At first, she denied reality. She didn't want to see herself as over-the-top as others did. But slowly she began to take notice of the effect she was having on her colleagues. She paid attention to eye contact and body language. She began to read a room.

She adjusted the way she showed up. She began to sit back, take in her environment and wait to speak when she had something valuable to contribute. She even wrote herself a message in her notebook before every meeting. It said: *why am I talking?*

With self-awareness, effort and perseverance, she was able to make a positive turnaround.

So, be brave. Look deeply at yourself. Notice how others respond to you. Is there a chance you're mistaking obnoxiousness for confidence or presence?

Here's my obnoxiousness self-check system.
Use it wisely.

1 Do you find a way to share in credit for successes you weren't very involved in?

2 Do you tend to speak far more than others in meetings?

3 Do you often correct other people?

4 Is your voice louder than average?

5 Are other people laughing at your jokes ... or are you the only one laughing?

6 When you're speaking, notice other people's facial expressions. Do they seem relaxed and at ease? Or tense and distracted?

7 When people ask you questions, is their tone of voice warm, supportive and enthused? Or somewhat abrasive or tired?

One of the most effective ways to gain self-awareness in this area is to video record yourself leading a meeting. Of course, you would need to seek permission from your attendees. Not doing so would be ... obnoxious.

When you watch the video later, have the self-check list handy and just be totally real with yourself. These can be easy habits to adjust when you become aware of them.

The Significance of Style

When it comes to being an Ultimate Executive, style has little to do with the brand of your suit.

It comprises everything about how you physically show up in the world.

Do you come to work looking rumpled and unkempt? Do you rush ungracefully into meetings, disorganized and harried? When you speak, do you ramble or second-guess yourself?

As superficial as style may seem, it speaks volumes to other people. Decision-makers factor in these physical cues usually without any consciousness that they're doing it. They're unwittingly using these factors to weigh how much they can trust you, how much you can handle.

Even someone with great substance and credibility can find their career limited by lack of style. They may rise quickly through the tiers of management, but struggle to garner the support and collaboration it takes to succeed at an executive level.

Simple things like body posture can communicate insecurity. Less confident people tend to make themselves small, particularly when they feel pressure to perform. Confident people tend to take up more space in the room, conveying a sense of assuredness to everyone around.

The basics of style are being organized, put-together and calm; speaking with authority; and using confident body posture.

Don't make the mistake of dismissing your style. It's communicating something about who you are. The question is, it is saying what you want it to?

Grace Under Pressure

If you tend to find curve balls amusing rather than annoying, chances are you've got situational agility.

This is one of the most telling signs of an Ultimate Executive. It's your ability to be gracious, articulate and composed under pressure. And to instantly draw on your wealth of knowledge to answer tough questions or solve urgent problems.

If you have situational agility, no one sees you break a sweat. If you're called to the podium half an hour sooner than expected or your laptop crashes as you take the stage, you deliver a kick-ass speech regardless.

If a major failure happens with your biggest customer, your reassuring demeanor and expert advice save the relationship.

People with this ability read individuals and situations quickly and accurately. They know when to speak and when to listen. They understand the dynamics in the room and adjust their behavior and tone accordingly.

Developing this skill is an exercise in deepening your intuition. It requires getting outside of your own head and the worries within it.

This is an ability you can continually advance over the course of your life, and as an Ultimate Executive, I encourage you to make this a mission. This skill will not just increase the caliber of your leadership, it will enhance your experience of life.

Presence

LEADING QUESTION

Do people see me the way I want them to?

Part Four:

ADVICE FOR
YOUR JOURNEY

It's About Them

It's simple. Ultimate Executives help other people be great. Your job is to create an atmosphere that fosters excellence.

The corporate world is a stressful, angst-ridden place because leaders fail to believe that people perform their best when they are valued.

But really it's obvious. Of course people are more effective when they know the ground beneath them is solid. They can focus. They can innovate. They can grow.

To create a healthy environment, you'll need to respect the power and autonomy of your team members. Sometimes this will mean letting people fail so they can learn a crucial lesson. Sometimes it will mean pushing just enough to let them soar.

These decisions are in your hands. You'll need to judge carefully what each moment requires. Let gut instinct, compassion and humility be your guides.

Ultimate Executives are highly intuitive about 3 things:

When to Shut Up: Other people will have their own methods of doing things that may look quite different from yours. Different is not worse. Know when to let others be. Also, know when others have more expertise than you and let their voices reign.

When to Walk Away: Some things are not yours to fix. You will spend your days resolving conflict and solving other people's problems if you don't know when to walk away. Know when it's appropriate to leave an issue unresolved for other people to manage.

When to Step in: These moments come in several forms. For example, when the risk you see is too great to just walk away and let someone learn their own lesson. Or when you see someone is pushing themselves to the point of no return and will hit burnout soon. Or, most importantly, when something inappropriate is taking place and needs to be stopped. Your executive job is a form of diplomacy. It's not your role to provide every answer. Your role is to read people and situations, and respond in a way that lets them grow.

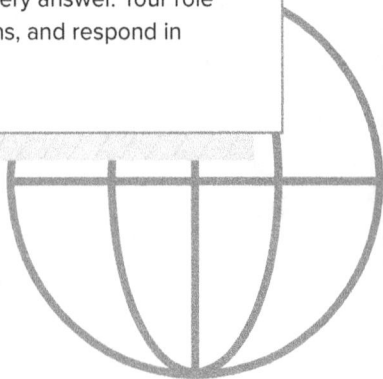

Everyone Profits

Congratulations. You've arrived at the end of this treatise on executive leadership. Now you're ready to approach your role with a fresh perspective.

I truly believe no matter how experienced you are, you can make an even bigger impact by living and breathing these skills every day.

Don't let them be concepts floating in your brain. They can only change your reality if you take action.

Be sure to use all 6 skills in equal measure. They are most potent as an integrated system.

You wouldn't be where you are today if you didn't want to live up to your biggest potential and create significant success for yourself and others.

So don't stop now. I suspect your possibilities are even bigger than you know.

My parting words of advice are:

> Let everyone be awesome.

> When you believe you're thinking big, think bigger.

> Don't let troublemakers poison your well. Fire fast.

> Be a leader of substance and integrity above all else.

Get out there. Make an impact.

Lisa

P.S. I love feedback. Please share your thoughts directly with me at:
lisa@lisamartininternational.com

Afterword

May I make a suggestion?

If you found this book of value, consider bringing the leadership development program, **LEAD ADVANCED: 6 Skills to Be the Ultimate Executive,** to your organization.

Just like this book, **LEAD ADVANCED** offers pragmatic skills to help leaders willing to assume the challenge of leading others to success. It's designed to help leaders transition their capacity and skills to an executive level.

Program participants learn advanced people skills, big-picture thinking and how to meet executive-level demands. It's ideal for mid- and senior-level leaders.

LEAD ADVANCED is a flexible, turnkey licensing solution that comes with all the tools required to cultivate high-impact, thriving leaders.

In other words, you get a proven program with all the training materials you need, including online 360 assessments, facilitator guides, workbooks, PowerPoint Decks, posters and, of course, this book.

And you have the freedom to deliver **LEAD ADVANCED** your way on your schedule.

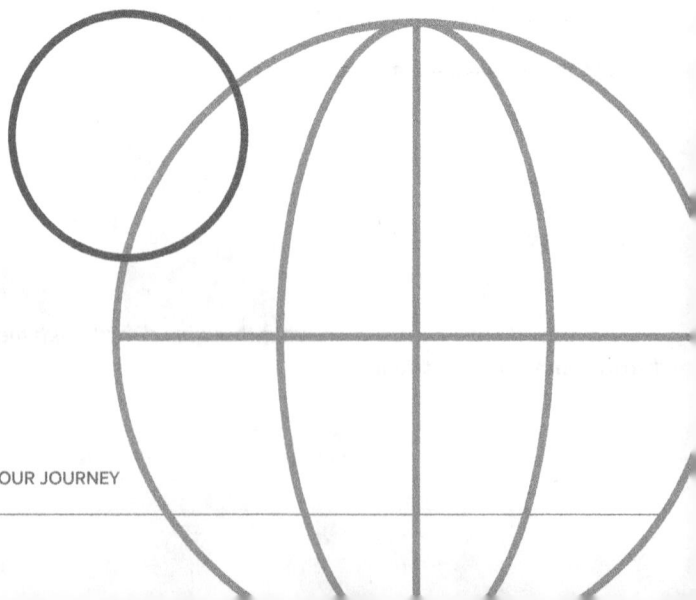

Acknowledgments

I was 30 years old when I was catapulted to an executive role. I went from running a 4-person agency to becoming the youngest partner in a national firm with more than 300 employees.

I sat at the partners' table with a roster of esteemed professionals, most of whom were 10 - 20 years my senior. I was responsible for improving profits, growing my local team and managing a national division.

I will tell you candidly, when I signed the agreement, I had no understanding of how much I'd taken on. I just leapt.

Lucky for me, I'm a learner. And believe me, I learned from everyone: my partners, the division heads, the finance people, and most significantly, my own team.

And so now, I thank them all. My understanding of how to elevate oneself to an executive level came from all of these gracious people. From them, I learned about the importance of being in service to others.

In more recent years as a leadership coach, I've continued learning from my many and varied leadership clients, watching as they each create massive impact in their own way. I thank all of you for letting me be your guide on the path of executive leadership.

This rather incomplete list of authors have influenced, informed and inspired my thinking on executive leadership: Marcus Buckingham, Brené Brown, Michael Bungay Stanier, Dr. Henry Cloud, Nancy Duarte, Seth Godin, Marshall Goldsmith, Daniel Goleman, Sheryl Sandberg, Susan Scott and Tom Rath.

I honor amazing leaders, present and past, who dared to think big and create impact. These include Peter Drucker, Bill Gates, Oprah Winfrey, Arianna Huffington and Roger L. Martin (no relation).

And finally, I thank you, reader. It's people like you, who desire excellence and personal development, who make this world a better place.

About the Author
Lisa Martin, PCC

Lisa Martin has made it her mission to help companies keep and cultivate leaders. She's the creator of the **Lead + Live Better**™ leadership programs; author of 5 books, including the bestselling **Briefcase Moms**; and a seasoned speaker, facilitator and executive coach.

For the past 15 years Lisa has designed and delivered leadership programs for PwC, TELUS, Vancouver Canucks, HSBC and UBC, to name a few.

Her powerful, easy-to-use **Lead + Live Better**™ turnkey leadership licensing solutions empower organizations to cultivate amazing leaders at every level.

She has coached thousands of people on the art of thriving as a leader and in life, and counseled companies on building leadership capacity.

As a speaker, Lisa is sought by international conferences, corporations and universities. She's known for her fun, straight-shooting speaking style and her intuitive sense for her audience.

She does all this as the founder of **Lisa Martin International**, a boutique leadership development firm with global scope, which equips organizations to deliver powerful leadership development in-house.

Lisa lives in North Vancouver with her husband, spirited teenaged son and two cats that act like toddlers.

You can find her at: **lisamartininternational.com**

"It's simple. Ultimate Executives help other people be great."

Lisa Martin

Cornerview Press
Box 30075
North Vancouver, BC
Canada V7H 2Y8

Edited by Jacqueline Voci
Cover and text design by Melissa Hicks & Melanie Iu
Cover image by Getty Images
Author Photo by Linda Mackie

ISBN 978-0-9734560-2-8

Library of Congress information is available on request.

The examples I've used in this book reflect the stories I've been privileged to share in my work as a leadership coach. To respect my clients' privacy, I have changed their names and other identifying details.

lisa MARTIN

LEAD+LIVE BETTER

Lisa's Lead+Live **Better**™ programs deliver advanced leadership and life skills in a fun, intuitive and straight-shooting way.

LEAD

6 Skills to Be a RockStar Leader

LEAD advanced

6 Skills to Be the Ultimate Executive

LEAD for women

Briefcase Moms

LEAD+LIVE

6 Practices to Live Bigger

LEAD+LIVE advanced

6 Practices to Master the Art of Thriving

lisamartininternational.com